How to Write Essays:

A Guide for Mature Students Who Have Forgotten How

KATE SCOTT

CONTENTS

INTRODUCTION

Essay writing is something that every student has to do, but writing good essays can be difficult. This book aims to help you with writing essays that will achieve good marks and help you towards your qualification.

While this book is a companion volume to *'Distance Learning and Mature Students: A Guide for Studying with The Open University'*, and is aimed at mature students who are returning to learning after a long hiatus, I hope it will also be of value to students in high school and those starting university.

1 WHAT IS AN ESSAY?

According to dictionary definitions, as essay is a short piece of writing on a particular subject.

Practically every course a student embarks on will require the writing of essays, whether for coursework and/or examinations. There are no rules to how many words an essay should contain, but usual essay lengths vary between 1,000 and 5,000 words. However, whatever the required length, all essays have the same structure in common. They must contain:

- An introduction
- Body paragraphs
- A conclusion
- A bibliography / reference section

What are tutors looking for?

Not only do essays have a defined structure, but they also have defined criteria of what they should demonstrate and achieve.

In your essay, your tutor (or whoever marks it) is going to be looking for:

- Understanding - they want you to show that you have understood the course material for the subject of the essay.

- Linking - they want you to identify and make links between the course material and the evidence you use to support your argument or points for your essay.

- Evaluating - they want you to weigh the evidence, judge its worth, and reach a conclusion.

Types of essay

There are three types of essays: descriptive, analytical, and argumentative.

- Descriptive - perhaps the simplest to achieve, but also the easiest to overwrite. A descriptive essay requires you to simply give a step-by-step description of the essay question's subject.

- Analytical - this type of essay requires an in-depth exploration of the question's subject, and a logical and methodical examination of its inherent factors or elements.

- Argumentative - this type of essay requires you to support or refute a statement or claim made in the essay question.

2 ESSAY QUESTIONS

Very often, essay questions can be difficult to understand. It seems that the question setter has gone out of their way to make it as confusing and incomprehensible as possible. It is, therefore, vital that you work out exactly what the question is asking you to do. You work this out by identifying the keywords or phrases in the question.

For example, which is the keyword in the following question?

Discuss the changing role of the hero in English literature.

The keyword here is 'Discuss'.

How about this one?

Analyse the character of the Red Cross Knight in Spenser's Faerie Queene.

The keyword here is 'Analyse'.

And lastly.

Othello escapes justice, but regains his honour by committing suicide. Do you agree with this statement?

The key phrase here is 'Do you agree?', with additional keywords of 'justice', 'honour', and 'suicide'.

Below is a list of the most common keywords and phrases that occur in academic essays.

- Analyse - Methodically examine the subject of the question, explain, and interpret.

- Compare - Describe similarities and differences between two or more subjects, sometimes demonstrating a preference for one or the other.

- Contrast - Describe the differences between two or more subjects.

- Describe - Give a detailed account of the subject in question.

- Discuss - Consider a subject, then define, and explain whichever argument you take in support or rejection of it.

- Examine - Describe a subject in detail, but not necessarily make a judgement or argument.

- Explore - Similar to 'examine', but requires a wider range of points.

- Evaluate - Make a judgement about a (critic's) opinion or subject.

- Refute - Use evidence to prove an argument or a statement is untrue.

If you are struggling with the complex language used in a question, try putting it into your own words to make it clearer. Use a thesaurus to find alternative meanings of words. Very often, a question can be simplified in this way, but be aware that you could subtly alter the meaning and premise of the question, thus affecting your essay answer.

It is important to keep the essay question, either the original or your own paraphrased version, in your mind as you write your essay, to ensure that you are providing an answer with every word.

The language of essays

Essays need to be written using a formal language, that is an academic language.

For example, you cannot use the same type of language you use to write blogs. In most cases, essays need to be de-personalised, with only questions that ask for an opinion permitting the use of the personal pronoun, I.

However, be wary of using complex language in an attempt to prove how clever you are. Essays should celebrate clarity, so you need to write using language that clearly, yet fully, expresses what you are trying to say. In other words, don't use long words when shorter ones will make your point more clearly.

Also, avoid using jargon and contractions. Imagine that your essay is being read by people who have no previous knowledge of the subject to avoid jargon use, and do not use 'don't', 'can't', 'shouldn't', etc., use 'do not', 'cannot', 'should not' instead. Finally, avoid waffle. It can be tempting to pad out an essay that has fallen short of the necessary word count by turning simple statements into more complex ones. Rather than do this and risk losing marks, find more points to include, or write better, fuller arguments for your essay.

Finally, never start sentences with 'and', 'but', or 'because'. Use instead 'moreover' or 'in addition', 'however', and 'due to'.

Making transitions

To achieve a smooth follow-on, or transition, between paragraphs, you will need to use particular words and phrases.

These include:

- However
- Therefore
- Nonetheless
- Nevertheless
- Despite this
- In addition
- Moreover
- To conclude
- In conclusion

These words and phrases will help to link your essay's paragraphs together.

Reading sources

Depending on your course, you may have several research resources available to you. These will include textbooks, critical essays, journals, and other printed and online articles.

Wherever you source the evidence used in your essay, it is vital that you make a bibliographic record of it, using whatever referencing system is used by your university and do this while you are actually reading them. There is nothing worse than trying to find a reference for a quotation you have used in your essay when you can't remember which book or journal you took it from.

Note taking

Once you have read and fully understood the essay question, you need to start gathering your evidence.

There is no 'best' way to make notes, as every person assimilates information differently.

However, there are some tried and tested methods. These include brainstorming, highlighting important and relevant passages in textbooks, making marginal annotations, and jotting down one-word or key phrases in a notebook.

Your notes for your essay can begin with what you already know. Then you can begin looking elsewhere for inspiration and evidence to back up your argument. However, beware of accumulating too much information that is only tangential to your core argument. Keep the essay question in mind at all times and restrict yourself to sources that deal directly with it.

Brainstorming can be an effective tool for generating ideas, especially helpful if you don't know where to start with your essay and you are staring at a blank page or screen.

To brainstorm, all you need do is take a sheet of paper (A4 size is fine), and in the middle, write the word/s that best describe the essay question's subject matter. With this one word or phrase, you then write down everything that comes to mind, and I do mean everything. Much of what you come up with will be irrelevant or extraneous to your needs, but there will be some words and phrases that will spark an idea, as well as the creative side of your brain.

3 THE ESSAY WRITING PROCESS

The essay writing process involves the follow stages:

- Reading and understanding the question.
- Reading the essay guidance.
- Reviewing the relevant chapters in the course books.
- Establishing your argument and gathering evidence.
- Creating an essay plan.
- Writing your first draft.
- Polishing your first draft to turn it into a

second draft.

- Reviewing your second draft.

- Submitting your final draft.

Structuring your essay

The best way to begin writing an essay is to create an essay plan. This is how you can define and control the structure of your essay.

Work on the premise that each paragraph within the main body of your essay will deal with point or argument.

Your essay plan is the basis for your essay, but it should serve only as a guide rather than a hard and fast rule. Be prepared to adapt it as you write your first draft as new thoughts occur to you.

Regarding writing style:

- Use sentences of varying lengths.

- Use active rather than passive verbs.

- Use positive language rather than negative.

To help you with this, simply turn on the

grammar checker within Microsoft Word. This function will underline phrases in blue that it thinks has questionable grammar, and will often suggest alternative phrases.

Now let's break the essay down.

The introduction

The introduction is where you state the position or argument you are going to take in the essay. Think of it as 'signposting', letting the reader know where your argument will be taking them.

There are certain elements your introduction should contain. These are:

- A definition of the question's key words/phrases to establish what is being asked of the writer.
- Your interpretation and understanding of the essay question.
- The nature of your evidence and why you

have chosen to focus on them.

- Follow with how they will be used to justify your argument.

This is an example of a poor introduction:

King Lear is a play governed by ideas of feudalism and patronage. Feudalism was a legal and social system that evolved in Western Europe during the 8th and 9th centuries, in which vassals were protected by a lord in return for serving under him in war. Patronage was a later system, which developed as the royal court grew more sophisticated and hierarchically structured, and in which a patron rewarded a client, financially or otherwise, in return for service. To offer service meant becoming part of a wider family unit, complete with loyalties and obligations. It used a particular style of language, where service was commonly termed as love, and declarations of such were reciprocated by the patron with added promises of reward.

To start off with, this introduction is too long; at least one sentence needs to be shaved off to make it a more suitable length. Secondly, it promises very little, and gives the reader no idea how the question is going to be tackled. Instead, it gives a description of feudalism and patronage, which in itself is very good, but if used, would be more suitable in the body of the essay.

This is an example of a good introduction:

The full title of Shakespeare's text is 'The Tragedy of Macbeth', which suggests that this play is first and foremost a psychological portrait of a man's descent into evil, not a society's. However, Macbeth the man can be said to be emblematic of that society, and the play can be interpreted as a critique of a certain 'social sphere that all the characters inhabit' (Kerr, 2000, p. 119).

This introduction is a better length. It also clarifies the position that the writer is going to take, namely that the tragedy inherent in Macbeth is Macbeth's, not the society in which he lives, but that the writer will also consider that Macbeth should be viewed as a symbol of society.

The body

Ideally, each paragraph you write that comes

between the introduction and conclusion should contain one aspect of your argument. Each body paragraph's first sentence is the key sentence where you state your point. The sentences that follow then provide evidence to back this sentence up. The last sentence of the body paragraph should provide a relevant and neat segway into the following paragraph. Try to use a minimum of two support evidences per point.

Example of a poor body paragraph:

Far From the Madding Crowd is a Realist novel, in that Hardy sets it in an imaginary Wessex, but within a recognisable countryside and society. Hardy's artistic eye imbues the novel with highly descriptive and visual passages that lend credence to its Realist genre. Despite this, it has been a difficult novel to categorise, as it contains elements of Gothic, melodrama, sensation, romance and pastoral fiction. As an offshoot of the Realist genre, Germinal is an attempt to write in a Naturalistic vein.

The opening sentence in this paragraph merely describes how the novel conforms to a Realist genre and makes vague comments about descriptive and visual passages. It is unbalanced, with the novel Germinal only have a one-sentence entry without any explanation of genre.

Example of a good body paragraph:

Macbeth himself is not portrayed nobly in Polanski's film. The original text description of his soldierly courage is truncated, so we do not hear how Macbeth was 'Disdaining fortune' (1.2.17) when he faced the enemy and became 'valour's minion' (1.2.19), or how when he and Banquo were outnumbered, they fought even harder, and against the odds, won. The only time Macbeth shows even the slightest hint of nobility in Polanski's film is towards the end, when he knows that he can be conquered by Macduff, and yet refuses to yield. If he did so, he would have to pay homage to 'young Malcolm', and be 'baited by the rabble's curse'. (1.2.27-8), a reference to the symbolism of the bear.

The paragraph opens with a bold statement and the following sentences provide evidence to support the statement.

The conclusion

This is where you bring together your arguments by summarising them. They should re-iterate the essay question, perhaps mention further research avenues, and include a personal view or stance.

End the essay with a neat sentence, not one that ends too quickly and gives the reader the impression that you ran out of words.

Example of a poor conclusion:

In both plays, Shakespeare seems to identify an innate quality that makes a man worthy of being a master and equally exposes deficiencies of character and moral integrity in some of those masters. Despite this, by the end of both plays, some form of the natural order has been restored, with both masters and servants once more occupying their proper places.

This conclusion is very short and rather vague. It does not refer explicitly back to the essay question, nor does it suggest further research, or give a personal opinion.

Example of a good conclusion:

These novels deal with very different themes and situations, yet still contain elements worthy of comparison in their portrayal and perception of women being susceptible and societally answerable to the male gaze, as theorised by Wittenberg. However, I would maintain that there are more differences than similarities between the two novels. Zola's Naturalistic attempt to be a dispassionate observer means that womanhood is not fully explored, and there is little or no psychological depth to his portrayal of women in Germinal. Hardy achieves a much more satisfying examination, and despite Wittenberg's claim, I believe a less stereotypical portrait of womanhood.

Quotations

It is quite likely that you will use quotations in your essay. These must be used in such a way that the sentence flows naturally, as in this example:

Eleanor can be attractive without looking to attract, and can talk without 'exaggerated feelings of ecstatic delight or inconceivable vexation on every little trifling occurrence' (ibid.), thereby mocking the talk of Isabella.

Do not pad out your essay with long quotations if only a small part of the quotation is needed to support your argument. If you do need to use an extensive quotation, it should be typed out as a standalone paragraph rather than integrated into a sentence.

If you are using a quotation that contains two points that are relevant to your argument, but which are separated by a section that is not, then you can condense the quotation by using the ellipsis (...) as in this example below.

'Entirely characteristic of Hardy's composition, ...the presentation of characters who, unknowingly, are watched by others.'

All quotes should be contained within either double quotation marks (" "), or single quotation marks (' '), whichever you prefer, as long as you keep the style consistent.

Referencing

Of great importance is the referencing of relevant parts of your essays. Many universities use the Harvard system of referencing, which is an author and date system, acknowledging the materials that have been cited in the essay.

For example:

Ryan, K. (2000). Shakespeare: Texts and Contexts. Milton Keynes: The Open University.

Bibliographic details for books/eBooks should include:

- Author's surname and initials
- Publication date
- Book title
- Publishers name
- Place of publication
- Page number of specific info or quotations, if applicable

Bibliographic details for journals/magazines should include:

- Author's surname and initials
- Article title
- Journal/magazine title
- Journal/magazine volume and/or number
- Journal/magazine's article page numbers

Bibliographic details for information retrieved from a website:

- Author's surname and initials (if available)
- Publication date (or last revised date)
- Document title
- Title of complete work (if applicable)
- URL (website address)
- Date site was accessed

There may not be the need to put full references in against every quote. An essay will be full of quotes, many of them from the same book. If you have a paragraph that contains several quotes from the same book, instead of putting the full reference each time, you should simply put (ibid.) and if it is a quote from the same book but on a different page, (ibid. p.34) for example. 'Ibid' means the same as what came before. This is only the case within paragraphs. Every time a new paragraph is opened, any quotes contained within it must be considered as standalones, and full referencing given, at least in the first instance.

If you have read other books in research for your essay, but not quoted from them or referred to them in your text, you can still include them in your bibliography, but it is not necessary, perhaps not even advisable, as some tutors may mark you down for this.

Plagiarism

This is the copying of another person's work verbatim and you simply must not plagiarise in your essay. Such actions can at best lose you marks, and at worst, see your work, and perhaps even you, disqualified.

Always use your own words in your essay, and when you do use a quotation, make sure you give the appropriate reference, acknowledging the original source. The copying of ideas, whilst a little more difficult to prove, can also be considered plagiarism, so credit these too. For example, if you were writing a physics essay and mentioned the theory of relativity, you should name Einstein as the originator of the theory.

Format

Your essay should follow this format:

- Typed on one side of the page only
- Each page should have standard margins (use the default setting on your word processing software)
- Double spaced lines
- Indented paragraphs

Put the essay question at the top of the first page, ideally using bold and/or a different colour to distinguish it from your answer.

4 FIRST DRAFT

Okay, you've written an essay - you're done, right?

Wrong!

It is extremely unlikely that you will have written a well-argued, coherent essay in your first attempt, which means that your essay is not finished. It needs editing and polishing and with luck your first draft will be longer than your required word count, which gives you scope to remove unnecessary sections.

I have a tip for you. On your PC (I am going to assume that you are using Microsoft Word or similar for your essays), open up a blank document alongside your essay. Save this blank document as 'Discards', and use it to hold all the sections you remove from your essay by cutting and pasting. This way, if you do decide that you wanted them after all, all you need do is paste them back.

Go through your first draft, keeping the essay question uppermost in your mind. Check that each paragraph responds to the question and provides a coherent argument.

Look to refine your writing. Can a sentence be better phrased? Would a different word clarify your argument better? Be careful with this, however, and do not attempt to use fancy words when a simpler one does the job just as well.

Once you have a second draft that conforms to the word count and that you are happy with, leave it for a day or so that you can come back to it in a more objective frame of mind.

Go through your second draft, just as you did your first, polishing and refining. You may think that two drafts are enough, but there is always room for improvement. However, you will be constrained by deadlines, and regardless of how many drafts you do, just make sure your final essay is as good as you can make it in the time allowed.

Reviewing

When you have your final draft, you still need to go through it once more, this time checking for errors, not contents. You can do this yourself, or get a relative or friend to do it for you. If your essay is very long, it might be worth your while to hire a professional proofreader to check it over. Mistakes such as spelling errors, typos, poor grammar, and punctuation will lose you marks, so do what you have to do to ensure your essay is as error-free as possible.

Learning from feedback

As I said before, no essay is perfect and can always be improved upon, so when your essay is returned to you, your tutor will undoubtedly have found things wrong with it.

Review the comments your tutor makes, and if they expose flaws in your arguments and reasoning or find fault with your formatting or errors, take these on-board and apply them to your next essay.

Writing is a skill, one that takes practice. The more you write essays, the better and easier they will become.

5 SAMPLE ESSAYS

Women offer an alternative set of values to those which prevail in the male world. Discuss with reference to Othello and The Rover, bearing in mind the different genres of those plays.

Despite different genres, both Othello and The Rover, explore similar themes of love, jealousy, deception, duty and honour. Whilst loss of honour has fatal consequences in Othello, the principle and perception of honour is constantly being challenged in The Rover by both men and women.

Othello is a tragedy, the definition of which is the downfall of a noble person. Inherent in that nobility is the concept of honour. It is Cassio who demonstrates the worth of honour in a man's person. The loss of his lieutenancy degrades him, so that he feels he has suffered a bodily hurt 'past all surgery.' (Shakespeare, W., (2005) p. 51, 1.253). He describes what reputation, and by extension, honour, means to him and speaks for all men of his caste with 'I have lost the immortal part of myself, and what remains is bestial,' (ibid, ll.256-7). Ironically, it is in part the attempt to restore his honour that contributes to the death of Desdemona for her supposed loss of honour.

In this patriarchal society, it is Brabantio's right to expect obedience and duty in his daughter, as he demands of Desdemona, by asking 'Do you perceive in all this company/Where most you owe obedience?' (Shakespeare, W., (2005) p. 22 ll.179-180). Desdemona challenges this, not denying that she does owe obedience, but arguing that she has transferred it from her father to her husband, 'as my mother showed/To you, preferring you before her father,' (ibid. p.23, ll. 184-5). That Desdemona should take for a husband 'what she feared to look on!' (ibid. p.20, 1.98) seems not so galling to Brabantio as that the marriage should 't'incur a general mock,' (ibid. p.15, 1.69) and thus disgrace him in the eyes of his peers. It is in fact, Brabantio's parting words that sows the seed for Othello's later belief in his wife's adultery, by reminding Othello that Desdemona 'has deceived her father, and may thee.' (ibid. p.26, l.290).

Brabantio speaks true; Desdemona deceived him by keeping her wooing of Othello secret. It is easy for a modern audience to overlook just how rebellious and indeed courageous an act this elopement of Desdemona's is. She is willing to defy her father and Venetian society in order to 'love the Moor to live with him,' (Shakespeare, W., (2005) p.25, l.246)and her character is defined with 'My heart's subdued/Even to the very quality of my lord,' (ibid. ll.248-9). Desdemona denies her father the conventional right for him to decide her future, and chooses to place her obedience in the hands of her husband.

Emilia too, displays duty and obedience to her husband, Iago, most evident in her taking of the handkerchief. She does this for Iago who has 'been so earnest/To have me filch it,', (Shakespeare, W., (2005) p.70, ll.312-3) judging the act to be above her duty to her mistress, despite knowing that Desdemona will 'run mad/When she lack it,' (ibid. ll.316-7). These duties are only reversed when the extent of Iago's villainy is revealed. He orders her to 'hold your peace,' (ibid. p.128, l.216) and 'get you home,' (ibid. l.221), which Emilia refuses to do though 'men, and devils,.../..., all cry shame against me,' (ibid. ll.219-220) for disobeying her husband so.

The idea of women as property is demonstrated in Othello's killing of Desdemona. Believing his honour to be impugned and his heart betrayed, Desdemona has made Othello 'A fixed figure for the time of scorn/To point his slow unmoving finger at,' (Shakespeare, W., (2005) p.99, ll.53-4). In Othello's tortured mind, Brabantio's warning has come true and 'she must die, else she'll betray more men,' (Shakespeare, W., (2005) p. 118, l.6). Othello justifies Desdemona's death not as 'A murder,' but 'a sacrifice,' (ibid. p. 121, l.65) he must make. His error realised and his fall from nobility of soul and position complete, Othello suggests a fitting epitaph for him would be to be called 'An honourable murderer,' (ibid. p.131. l.291) for it was to restore his honour that Othello killed Desdemona. It is telling that it is for the murder and attempted murder of Roderigo and Cassio respectively that Othello is to be arrested, not for Desdemona's. It is therefore, we must assume, Othello's right to execute an adulterous wife, but not her supposed lover, re-enforcing the double standard. For Desdemona's part, even though she declares her innocence, she does not dispute her husband's right to act against her, begging 'Banish me, my lord, but kill me not,' (ibid. 121, l.79).

A comedy differs from a tragedy in that it is not required to be a psychological study, but rather a plot that contains a series of coincidences, mistaken identities along with other stock dramatic devices and that stock characters can be used, for example Belvile is the conventional lover, Blunt the fool, Willmore the rake. Despite this, The Rover covers many of the same themes as Othello and holds the same values. Whilst women play a passive role in Othello, women drive the action in The Rover.

Like Desdemona, the sisters Florinda and Hellena in The Rover challenge male authority to determine their own futures. Florinda declares of her father's intention to marry her off as 'I understand better what's due to my beauty, birth and fortune and more to my soul than to obey those unjust commands' (Behn, A., (2010) p.265, ll.18-20). Hellena seems most unfit for a nunnery, for she loves 'mischief strangely' (ibid. ll.21-2) and is 'resolved to provide myself ... a handsome proper fellow' (ibid. l31-2). Their father and brother ignore their natures and desires as being things of no consequence. It is here, in this opening scene, that the idea of women belonging to their male relatives as property is most notably demonstrated and shares this value with Othello.

To Pedro, though he acknowledges that Belvile is a 'young and fine' (Behn, A., (2010) p.266, l.70) gentleman, that alone cannot make him a suitable husband for Florinda, for he argues 'what jewels will that cavalier present you with? Those of his eyes and heart?' (ibid. l.71) They are evidently fortune enough for Florinda who loves Belvile. The husband that their father has chosen is a rich man, and Pedro bids Florinda to 'consider Don Vincentio's fortune, and the jointure he'll make you.' (ibid. ll.66-7). Meanwhile, Pedro's candidate for Florinda's hand, Antonio, is 'brave and young, and all that can complete the happiness of a gallant maid,' (ibid. p.267, ll.131-2) and Florinda herself admits that she has no valid argument against marrying him, for 'I've no defence against Antonio's love,/For he has all the advantages of nature,/The moving arguments of youth and fortune.' (ibid. ll.143-5).

Though they have similar personalities and desires, the different values that men and women hold are most notably demonstrated by Hellena and Willmore. Willmore asserts that he pursues 'love and beauty' (Behn, A., (2010) p.322, ll.411-2) and this is his excuse, or reason, for his unbridled lust. In true rake character, every woman he comes across he tries to have sex with, sometimes forcibly, as in the case with Florinda. Hellena seems to share this lust for physical pleasure, but she counters his arguments for pre-marital sex with the realities of what that would entail for a woman, with 'what shall I get? A cradle full of noise and mischief, with a pack of repentance at my back?' (ibid. ll.417-8). Women are forced to consider the consequences of their actions in a way men in this period are not obliged to. Belvile calls Willmore 'a rover of fortune, yet a prince aboard his little wooden world' (ibid. p.324, ll.468-9), meaning his ship, which is conveniently anchored off shore, ready for a speedy exit. Pedro, who has his sister's honour and future to consider, counters this with 'What's this to the maintenance of a woman of her birth and quality?' (ibid. l.470). It is important to note that it is only the possession of a fortune that enables Hellena to finally decide her own future and snare Willmore as a husband. Pedro is glad to be rid of her for he is now 'free from fears of her honour...I have been a slave to't long enough' (ibid. l.484-6), her honour being the keeping of her virginity until she is married. Men here are responsible for maintaining honour in their female relatives, for, as in Othello, any slur would taint them and it seems to be a heavy responsibility.

Here we have two plays, written eighty years apart, one written by a man, the other by a woman, one a tragedy, the other a comedy. Yet they both show that ideas of the passivity and subordination of women were, in part, misconceptions and that honour, or at least the appearance of honour, were paramount.

Shakespeare, of course, was unusual for his time in his understanding of womankind, but it is obvious from these two plays, that women and men did hold very different ideas about how they should be treated. What these two plays demonstrate is that men valued honour and the perception of honour, whilst women, while no less understanding of honour's worth and rewards, were prepared to make sacrifices and challenge society's rules to pursue independent desires.

Bibliography

Behn, A., The Rover in Owens, W.R. & Goodman, L., (ed.) (2010) Shakespeare, Aphra Behn and The Canon, The Open University, Milton Keynes, pp. 262-327

Owens, W.R. & Goodman, L., (2010) Shakespeare, Aphra Behn and The Canon, The Open University, Milton Keynes

Shakespeare, W., (2005) Othello, Penguin Books, London

Read the passage below from Pride and Prejudice (volume III, chapter 13) carefully several times. Then, in a continuous essay of not more than 1,000 words, analyse this passage, discussing how narrative voice and dialogue are important elements in the creation of meaning in the passage.

The passage opens with dialogue, spoken by Mrs Bennet, here referred to as 'his wife'. Austen does name her interlocutor in the second sentence, but referring to Mrs Bennet as an adjunct to her husband, 'demotes her dignity' and enables the narrator to establish an 'ironic distance' from Mrs Bennet (Morris, P. (2010) p.34).

Mrs Bennet is one of a few characters who do not change or evolve throughout the novel, and we therefore trust the narrator's original viewpoint of her, which in the first chapter was given as 'a woman of mean understanding, little information, and uncertain temper.'(Austen, J. (2008) p.3). This section of dialogue amply qualifies this opinion, for she makes assumptions based on little or no information – 'he has four or five thousand-a-year, and very likely more' - and her moods are transient, shifting quickly with each piece of news or change of fortune – 'Wickham, Lydia, were all forgotten. Jane was beyond competition her favourite child.' Of course, by this time, the reader knows that Mrs Bennet is a vulgar, comic figure, her 'garrulous'(ibid.) conversation frequently embarrasses her two eldest, and most sensible, daughters. The reader trusts nothing Mrs Bennet says.

The omniscient narrator, speaking in the third person, takes over. This is direct narrative, in that it is addressed to the reader. Austen dispenses with dialogue to 'tell' what has happened rather than 'show' by having the characters speak. Austen never wastes time on setting the scene, and by simply saying 'from this time', we are shown in summary how the engagement of Jane and Bingley affect the rest of the family. We are told how Mary and Kitty ask Jane for favours for when she is mistress of Netherfield. The adjectives used reinforce the sisters' natures – Mary 'petitions', showing her prim and formal character, whilst 'almost begs' shows Kitty's passionate, desperate nature.

Austen decides not to give the reader any of Jane and Bingley's conversations. We know they have them, for the narrator tells us so, using Elizabeth as the focaliser, for it is her opinions that are expressed. Neighbours who entice Bingley away from Longbourn are mockingly spoken of as being 'barbarous' and 'could not be enough detested,' undoubtedly the language of Elizabeth. By not putting this in direct speech, the effect is to suggest that this is a consensus of opinion throughout the Bennet family.

Jane's remarks, though harsher than we are used to from her, are still temperate. Jane realises she has been wrong, even naive, in her preference for Bingley's sisters, especially Caroline Bingley, yet she still has hopes of a future friendship, even though she acknowledges they cannot be 'what they once were'. Yet even here, when Jane has delighted Elizabeth with her 'unforgiving speech', she is showing that she is still under a misapprehension, for she does not realise that Miss Bingley expressed only a 'pretended regard' for her.

For the second time in this passage, Elizabeth, once again acting as the focaliser, withholds information from Jane about Darcy, the first being when Jane is speaking of her time in London and says that Bingley was ignorant of her being there, Elizabeth lies and says she 'suspected as much', when in truth she knows far more than she is telling Jane. This section makes use of free indirect speech, for Elizabeth's thoughts on the matter are conveyed without any dialogue being spoken; for example, 'Elizabeth was pleased to find' and 'she knew'.

Jane's next burst of dialogue, and burst it is, for no fewer than five exclamation points are used, allows the reader to have knowledge which is withheld from Jane. When Jane cries 'If there were but such another man for you!', we the reader knows that there is – Mr Darcy. This is an example of irony.

Yet again, Elizabeth deigns to enlighten Jane. She mocks herself by saying 'if I have very good luck, I may meet with another Mr Collins in time.' Elizabeth is always able to laugh at herself, but she is also pragmatic enough to know, despite mocking her mother's foolish behaviour in regard to finding husbands for her daughters, her future prospects, if she remains unmarried, are bleak indeed.

Another example of irony comes when the narrator informs the reader that Jane's engagement 'could not be long a secret'. We, the reader and the narrator, know that keeping such a secret would be the furthest thing from Mrs Bennet's desires. Mrs Bennet lets slip – 'privileged to whisper' - the news to her fellow gossip, Mrs Philips, and because we know Austen, and we believe in the characters she has created, we can surmise that Mrs Philips informs the rest of the neighbourhood with Mrs Bennet's tacit blessing, despite the assurance of it being 'without her permission'.

The final paragraph describes the Bennet's change of fortune in the eyes of their neighbours, who were only weeks before lamenting that family's 'misfortune' in the instance of Lydia and Wickham, but who now believe the

Bennet's to be 'the luckiest family in the world', because of Jane's engagement to Bingley. The wording 'pronounced' and 'proved' have legal overtones and Austen deliberately misuses them to show 'the fickleness of public opinion' and mock 'sentiment' (Gray, M. & Jeffares, A.N (2001) p.62).

Austen uses several different narrative techniques in this passage – narration, dialogue and indirect speech to further our understanding of character and plot. This type of writing, the use of multiple techniques that interact with one another, is termed a dialogic. A dialogic enables a writer to express different characters points of view and sometimes allows the reader to know their thought processes. The dialogue used here also expresses character. For example, for Mrs Bennet, the dialogue is rapid and divergent; for Jane, the language is serene and compassionate; for Elizabeth, pragmatic and guarded. Dialogue is not given to the secondary characters in this passage (Kitty, Mary, Mrs Philips) but their actions, related by the narrator, sum up what we, the reader, know of their characters perfectly.

Bibliography

Austen, J., (2008) Pride and Prejudice, Oxford, Oxford University Press,

Gray, M. & Jeffares, A.N (2001) York Notes Advanced - Pride and Prejudice, London, York Press

Morris, P., (2010) 'Reading Pride and Prejudice', in Walder, Dennis (ed.) The Realist Novel, Open University, pp. 31-60

'The narrative voice is an important element in the use of realist and non-realist techniques and conventions.' Discuss this statement with reference to one of the following novels: Frankenstein, Fathers and Sons, Great Expectations.

In the eighteenth century, a genre of novel known as bildungsroman emerged with the publication of Goethe's The Apprenticeship of Wilhelm Meister. A novel of this type is centred on the physical and emotional growth of an individual, beginning with his youth and expulsion from a family group arising from a conflict or crisis, followed by pursuit of the protagonist's ambitions and desires, leading to a resolution that results in a greater wisdom and maturity.

This follows the evolution of the novel, which were at one point marketed as 'histories', such as The History of Tom Jones, a Foundling and these were intended to be read as fictional autobiographies. This shows the move away from Romance, in which novels depicted a fantasy world and towards Realism, which attempted to mirror real life. Further examples appeared in the nineteenth century; Jane Eyre and David Copperfield. Dickens revisited the genre with Great Expectations, which follows 'the life of Pip, an anxious and guilt-ridden child, sensitive to the point of hysteria, and altogether a very queer, small boy.' (Ackroyd, P, (2002) p.459-460).

The narrative structure of Great Expectations follows a linear timeline. It is written in the first person, and is narrated by the adult Philip Pirrip, who introduces himself with astonishing brevity and straightforwardness by explaining the origins of his nickname, Pip. We have, therefore, a 'dual-narrative' perspective; the adult Pip, the story's narrator, relates events but describes them as they appeared to his younger self. This dual perspective is necessary to allow the adult Pip to reflect on his past life. A child narrator could not be expected to provide with any sincerity or value moral judgements about his behaviour, which was essential to a Victorian audience, who expected their fiction to be morally uplifting and were scandalised when it wasn't so. It also allowed the protagonist to step outside the confines of the plot and on occasion, appeal directly to the reader, for example, 'Pause, you who read this, and think for a moment...' (Dickens, C. (2008) p.66). This first-person viewpoint, whilst allowing the reader entry into the mind of the character, restricts the scope of the novel, for only scenes where the narrator is present can be related by him, for they are the only ones he can have firsthand knowledge of.

Pip is an unusual protagonist in that he is not a greatly sympathetic character. He is snobbish, unkind and resentful to people, we the reader, recognise he should be grateful to. This, of course, follows the bildungsroman motif, for it is necessary for Pip to evolve into a more mature and wise human being by the end of the novel. We, the reader, have to be objective about what we are being told, remembering that people and events are described to us as the young Pip sees them, and later, with moral judgements appended, by the adult Pip. Whilst doing this, the reader keeps in mind Pip's character (which is very human and therefore Realistic) and his flaws.

After a vivid description of the area in which Pip lives and a brief, unsentimental history of his family, both of which serve to reinforce the idea of Realism by their very ordinariness, the reader is launched into the crisis of Pip's childhood and the catalyst for the plot, the meeting with the escaped convict Magwitch. The immediacy of the first-person narrator can seduce the reader into forgetting that the adult Pip is a 'fictional construct as much as the boy Pip.' (Walder, D. (2010), p.143) and of course, Realism as a genre is itself a construct.

When Dickens came up with the idea for Great Expectations, he described it as a 'very fine, new, grotesque idea.' (Douglas-Fairhurst, R

(2008) p.ix). He meant Grotesque in its original sense, that of the 'tragi-comic', and the humorous tone of the narrative voice demonstrates this. For example, 'I earnestly expressed my hope that he wouldn't' (Dickens, C. (2008) p.4) is the adult Pip's ironic version of the young Pip's response to Magwitch's terrible threat to eat his fat cheeks. Later in the novel, when Pip's great expectations have been tainted by the revelation of the identity of his benefactor, and when he has emotionally matured, Magwitch inspires first revulsion and then pathos in the adult Pip; 'my repugnance to him had all melted away...' (ibid. p.408).

To return to the opening scene as an example of the Grotesque, we see Magwitch for the first time as Pip the child saw him, so we are treated to a nightmarish description of the convict, who 'limped, and shivered, and glared and growled.' (ibid. p.4) Magwitch is animal-like in his growling and lip-licking and here is the grotesque element that Dickens spoke of, for another definition of the Grotesque is the mutation of human elements into animal or plant life. It is probable that, to an adult eye, Magwitch would be more pitiable than fearsome.

This scene also embodies Gothic tradition, a genre which combines horror and romance. The horror is evident in this scene; Pip sees Magwitch lumbering away among the nettles and brambles of the churchyard, looking 'in my young eyes as if he were eluding the hands of the dead people, stretching up cautiously out of their graves, to get a twist upon his ankle and pull him in.' (ibid. p.6). A Romantic element is to be found in the strangeness of the situation. Gothic Romance is also exhibited in the plot convolutions, the improbabilities of Pip's world; for example, Mr Jagger's working for both Miss Havisham and Magwitch, (surely two characters at either end of the social scale) and even having employed Molly, the mother of Estella, who is of course linked to them all. Pip's world is very small and inter-connected.

Miss Havisham is another Gothic, one could argue even Grotesque, creation, a wraith-like creature, emotionally and mentally damaged by her past, who wanders around her house, which is as decayed as she, corrupting the natures of those she invites in. Pip calls her 'the strangest lady I have ever seen,' and he goes on to describe her as having 'sunken eyes' and a body 'shrunk to skin and bone.' (ibid. p.52) She resembles a 'ghastly waxwork' and he remembers a skeleton he has seen and when looking upon Miss Havisham he now imagines that 'wax-work and skeleton seemed to have dark eyes that moved and looked at me.' (ibid. pp 52-53). By using this kind of language, where the horror is exaggerated because it is the viewpoint of a child, Dickens manages to conjure up an image of Miss Havisham almost as a walking corpse.

The house is a symbol of its occupant; the 'windows had been walled up' (ibid. p.50), signifying Miss Havisham's refusal to see the outside world and keep outsiders outside. The objects around Miss Havisham signify the state of her mind – 'the stopped clock, the wedding garments and the closed room...provide...an indirect expression of Miss Havisham's mental condition.' (Walder, D. (2010), p.149).

Trabb's Boy and Orlick could also be viewed as Gothic creations, if one were to think of them as physical manifestations of the darker aspects of Pip's character. Orlick could be a 'surrogate for Pip's own suppressed feelings of rage and hurt,' (Ackroyd, P, (2002) p.460), but tempered by Pip's innate and omnipresent guilt, fearing the weapon used against his sister is the file he gave to Magwitch; 'It was horrible to think that I had provided the weapon...' (Dickens, C. (2008) p.110).

Trabb's Boy publicly ridicules Pip's pretensions to gentility. Trabb's Boy exposes Pip's own latent fears that expensive clothes and sudden wealth do not make a gentleman; 'my first decided experience of the stupendous power of money, was, that it had morally laid upon his back, Trabb's boy,' (ibid. p.138) and 'my position was a distinguished one, and I was not at all dissatisfied with it, until Fate threw me in the way of that unlimited miscreant, Trabb's boy.' (ibid. p.224).

One could argue the ending of the novel is Realistic, as there is no Romantic happy ending; Dickens leaves the reader to wonder whether Pip and Estella will marry. Pip and Estella are reunited in friendship at the conclusion, after they both have endured trials, as Estella says 'I have been bent and broken, but – I hope – into a better shape', (ibid. p.442) but Dickens had originally written them as getting married, but he thought this was too sentimental, too Romantic an ending, and changed it to them walking away together - 'I took her hand in mine, and ...I saw the shadow of no parting from her.' (ibid).

To conclude, Great Expectations cannot be pigeon-holed into any one genre. Dickens did not want his fiction to fall into a 'literal and catalogue-like' section of literature; he preferred to give his writing 'a fanciful treatment' (Walder, D. (2010), p.146) and that meant mixing literary devices and conventions. To contemporary writers, such as George Eliot and Elizabeth Gaskell, who were struggling to make the novel an acceptable 'high' art form, this kind of approach demeaned the novel and Dickens's work was considered 'low' and Dickens himself merely a 'great entertainer.' (ibid. p.147).

Bibliography

Ackroyd, P., (2002) Dickens, London, Vantage

Brooks, P., (1996) 'Repetition, Repression, and Return: The Plotting of Great Expectations' in Connor, Stephen (ed.) Charles Dickens, Longman Critical Readers, London, Addison Wesley Longman Limited, pp. 34-58

Dickens, C., [1860] (2008) Great Expectations, Oxford, Oxford University Press,

Douglas-Fairhurst, R (2008) 'Introduction' in Dickens, Charles Great Expectations, Oxford, Oxford University Press, pp. viii-xxxvii

Eagleton, T., (1996) 'Ideology and Literary Form: Charles Dickens' in Connor, Stephen (ed.) Charles Dickens, Longman Critical Readers, London, Addison Wesley Longman Limited, pp. 151-158

Hobsbaum, P,. (1972) 'Great Expectations (1861)' in Hobsbaum, Peter A Reader's Guide to Charles Dickens, London, Thames and Hudson, pp. 221-242

Walder. D., (2010) 'Reading Great Expectations' in Walder, Dennis (ed.) The Realist Novel, Open University, pp. 135-166

A210 (2010) Audio CD1, Approaching Literature: The Language of Realism, OU, 94YA 9938 LJO

The Electronic Labyrinth (2010), Realism and the Realist Novel, available from http://elab.eserver.org/hfl0254.html (Accessed 28th October 2010)

Georgia Southern University (2010), A Glossary of Literary Gothic Terms, available from http://personal.georgiasouthern.edu/~dougt/goth.html (Accessed 29th October 2010)

Wikipedia (2010), Narrative Mode, available from http://en.wikipedia.org/wiki/Narrative_mode (Accessed 29th October 2010)

Wikipedia (2010), Bildungsroman, available from http://en.wikipedia.org/wiki/Bildungsroman (Accessed 3rd November 2010)

Write an essay of 1,500 words, in which you compare William Wordsworth's The Prelude, Book 1, ll.306-72 (Romantic Writings: An Anthology pp. 113-14), with one of the following poems on the theme of childhood:

The Schoolboy, The Echoing Green, Nurse's Song

'The Prelude' is an intensely personal and autobiographical poem. It is both lyrical, reflecting the thoughts and feelings of Wordsworth, and a narrative poem, in that it recounts scenes from his life. It is a poem about memory and how the passage of time can colour recollections.

In the section we are concerned with, the poet is recounting a time during his childhood when he identified so closely with Nature, that he became a part of it. 'The Prelude' is written in blank verse using an iambic pentameter, which is ideal for the reminiscing tone of the poem.

The tone of the passage opens quietly, with a description of a seemingly idyllic childhood in which Wordsworth is a child of Nature, 'foster'd' (l. 307) by her. Wordsworth employs plant imagery to portray his upbringing, describing himself as a seed with Nature nurturing his 'soul' (l.306). He continues with this metaphor, when describing his move to a new home, as being 'transplanted' (l.310). The use of words such as 'seed' (l. 306) and 'transplanted' (l.310) indicate the extreme youth of the poet. Nature taught him his lessons using both 'beauty' and 'fear' (l.307), Wordsworth acknowledging that whilst Nature is beautiful, she is also dangerous.

There is a transcendental aspect to this passage, especially with the change in tone at line 317, where it becomes almost savage. Gone is the tranquil language of the earlier lines, and there is now a speed and urgency to the events being recounted. The child is no longer taking nocturnal winter walks, wandering 'half the night among the Cliffs/And the smooth Hollows,' (ll. 315-16), but has become an agent of death, a 'fell destroyer' (l. 319) who goes armed with traps - 'springes' (l.318) to catch the running woodcocks. There is an echo of Shakespeare in these lines – 'springes to catch woodcocks,' (Shakespeare, W. (1994) p.1,087, l.114). Nature has, by example, taught the boy to hunt, and his desires - 'In thought and wish' (l.317) - are predominantly predatory.

The 'scudding away from snare to snare' (l.320) conjures up an image of the boy laying his traps in a hurry, running low across 'the heights,' (l.319). Wordsworth uses repetition to convey this sense of urgency and the use of enjambment in these particular lines reinforces this sense – 'hurrying on,/Still hurrying, hurrying onward,' (ll. 321-22). There is a breathlessness in the language with the 'and almost, as it seem'd,' (l.345).

My initial reading of this passage led me to believe it was the boy's spirit or his dream-self that was engaging on these nocturnal wanderings, for what would a nine year old boy be doing alone on the vales and hollows at night? However, this boy does appear to have a real presence in this wilderness. He steals from traps already laid – 'the captive of another's toils/Became my prey,' (ll. 328-29). This self-confessed undeserved bounty means that the boy, at least in his imagination, in turn becomes the hunted and that the hills have become living things, with 'Low breathings coming after me,' (l. 331). The boy has become afraid. In the spring, the boy is still a 'plunderer' (l.337), scaling the 'lonesome peaks,' (l.338) of the country, this time in daylight. Again, birds are his object and he admits his quest is 'mean' and 'inglorious,' (ll. 340-341), but Nature approves of his actions because whilst he is attacked 'by the blast which blew amain,' (l.346), he is seemingly supported and 'suspended' by the wind as he hung about the 'slippery rock' (l. 344) and 'naked crag,' (l. 347). The wind is alive to the boy and communicates with him, making a 'strange utterance' (l. 349) and invading his ears, astounding him with its power to move 'the clouds!' (l. 351). The last four and a half lines of this stanza provide a link into the last, more philosophic section.

There is again an echo of Shakespeare, namely 'Hamlet' with the title character's philosophical musing on 'What a piece of work is a man!' (Shakespeare, W (1994) p.1,096, ll.301-02). Like Hamlet, who understands man to be a complicated creation, 'noble in reason', 'infinite in faculties', 'in action...like an angel', 'in apprehension, how like a god!' (ibid. ll.302-05) and revels in it, Wordsworth muses on the complicated structure of man's mind – 'a dark/Invisible workmanship,' (ll. 353-54). He believes there to be a harmony, similar to music, that 'reconciles/Discordant elements, and makes them move/In one society,' (ll. 354-56). There is a reverence here for Nature, an almost pagan worship of the natural world. Wordsworth seems to be saying that the only education a child needs is that of Nature, through whom God speaks.

Unlike 'The Prelude', the structure of Blake's 'The Schoolboy' is uniform, the poem composed of six stanzas, comprising five lines each. The rhythm is different with the stanzas written mainly in iambic tetrameter with variations. There is also rhyme in this poem, in a regular ABABB fashion, in complete opposite to the blank verse of 'The Prelude'. Unlike 'The

Prelude', which is a reminiscence, 'The Schoolboy' is an appeal and asks questions of its reader.

Upon first reading, Blake seems to be agreeing with Wordsworth that Nature is the best teacher. The poem opens with something akin to a pastoral idyll. Birds are singing, Blake is singing and a huntsman is blowing his horn in the distance. It is a very positive opening, written from the point of view of the adult poet but again, like 'The Prelude', there is a suggestion of danger in the country with the inclusion of 'the distant huntsman' (1.3).

The 'But' (1.6) of the opening line of the second stanza abruptly changes the tone of the piece. Here, we are moved from natural surroundings to the environs of the schoolroom, and we are meant to contrast the mournful tone of 'Oh, it drives all joy away!' (1.7) with the happy line 'Oh, what sweet company!' (1.5) from the first stanza. Blake's sympathies are with the 'little ones' (1.9), the children who are stuck inside a school on a 'summer morn,' (1.6) working under the 'cruel eye' (1.8) of a schoolmaster. The school environment - 'learning's bower' (1.14) - is 'worn through' (1.15) and the schoolmaster's eye is 'outworn,' (1.8), conveying an idea of a tired and exhausted institution. The implication that follows is how can children be inspired in such surroundings?

This type of education depresses Blake and gives him an 'anxious hour' (l.12) and, though he wants to, he cannot 'take delight' (l.13) in his own studies.

From the fourth stanza onwards, the poem becomes a series of rhetorical questions for the reader. Blake employs imagery in these final three stanzas, comparing children to objects in nature. Blake firstly uses the image of a bird, who because of its cage cannot sing freely. The boy then becomes like the bird, having a 'tender wing' (l.19) instead of an arm. In the fifth stanza, children are referred to with plant imagery. The children are 'buds' (l.21), 'blossoms' (l.22) and 'tender plants' (l.23). The final stanza continues with the plant metaphor and is concerned with the fruits of education. Blake believes that the education gained outside of the schoolroom during the summer months in effect provides a store of experience and education that can be harvested during the 'blasts of winter' (l.30).

Both poems are about lessons being taught and experience gained and the best way in which this is done. Wordsworth fully believes that Nature, in her harsh way, is the greatest teacher. Blake, whilst not eschewing a conventional education, posits the theory that less strict discipline, allowing more freedom of thought, is a better education. He appeals to parents not to forsake natural learning altogether by replacing it with a formalized education. Man oppresses the spirit with his shutting out of nature and discourages development. Blake is saying whilst Nature is being bountiful, man should take every opportunity to glory in it. Unlike Wordsworth, Blake sees Nature's lessons and schoolroom teaching working together in harmony.

All the alleged cruelty in 'The Schoolboy' comes from man, in direct contrast to 'The Prelude' excerpt, where the boy is the only human presence and is taught cruelty by Nature. In 'The Prelude', Nature teaches predation and cruelty to the boy, who learns that lesson and re-visits it upon Nature, thus fulfilling the natural cycle of life.

Blake idealises Nature in his poem – Wordsworth describes it with fear, love and awe. There is a real sense of worship in 'The Prelude', whereas Blake seems to view Nature as bringing enrichment to life.

Bibliography

Asbee, S., (2010) Approaching Poetry, The Open University, Milton Keynes

Blake, W., 'The Schoolboy' in Owens, W.R & Johnson, H,. (eds.) (1998) Romantic Writings:

An Anthology, The Open University, Milton Keynes, p.19

Bygrave, S. (ed) (1998) Romantic Writings, The Open University, Milton Keynes

Owens, W.R. & Johnson, H., b(eds.) (1998) Romantic Writings: An Anthology, The Open University, Milton Keynes

Shakespeare, W., 'Hamlet, Prince of Denmark' in (1994) Complete Works of Shakespeare, Harper Collins, Glasgow, pp.1079-1125

Wordsworth, W., 'The Prelude' in Owens, W.R & Johnson, H,. (eds.) (1998) Romantic Writings: An Anthology, The Open University, Milton Keynes, pp.113-114

FROM THE AUTHOR

I have a favour to ask...

I hope this guide has been of some help to you in your studies. If it has, I would be extremely grateful if you would post a review on Amazon and share it with your friends on Facebook and Twitter.

Thank you.

Kate Scott

ALSO AVAILABLE

Distance Learning and Mature Students:
A Guide for Studying with The Open University
By
Kate Scott

Available in paperback and eBook from Amazon

17933463R00038

Printed in Great Britain
by Amazon